P9-BXV-438

MT. PLEASANT PUBLIC LIBRARY
MT. PLEASANT, IOWA

DEMCO

CLEOPATRA

MT. PLEASANT PUBLIC LIBRARY
MT. PLEASANT. IOWA

Struan Reid

Heinemann Library
Chicago, Illinois

© 2002 Reed Educational & Professional Publishing
Published by Heinemann Library,
an imprint of Reed Educational & Professional Publishing,
Chicago, Illinois

Customer Service 888-454-2279

Visit our website at www.heinemannlibrary.com

All rights reserved. No part of this publication may be reproduced or transmitted in any form or by any means, electronic or mechanical, including photocopying, recording, taping, or any information storage and retrieval system, without permission in writing from the publisher.

Designed by Celia Floyd
Illustrated by Jeff Edwards and Joanna Brooker
Originated by Ambassador Litho Ltd
Printed in Hong Kong by Wing King Tong

06 05 04 03 02
10 9 8 7 6 5 4 3 2 1

Library of Congress Cataloging-in-Publication Data
Reid, Struan.
 Cleopatra / Struan Reid.
   p. cm. -- (Historical biographies)
Includes bibliographical references and index.
Summary: Presents an account of Cleopatra's life, from birth to death, and explores her impact on history and the world.
 ISBN 1-58810-565-2 (HC), 1-58810-998-4 (Pbk.)
 1. Cleopatra, Queen of Egypt, d. 30 B.C.--Juvenile literature. 2. Egypt--History--Greco-Roman period, 332 B.C.-640 A.D.--Juvenile literature. 3. Queens--Egypt--Biography--Juvenile literature. [1. Cleopatra, Queen of Egypt, d. 30 B.C. 2. Kings, queens, rulers, etc. 3. Women--Biography. 4. Egypt--History--Greco-Roman period, 332 B.C.-640 A.D.] I. Title. II. Series.
 DT92.7 .R4 2002
 932'.021'092--dc21

2001003660

Acknowledgments
The author and publishers are grateful to the following for permission to reproduce copyright material:
Cover photograph: AKG
p. 4 University of Glasgow Hunterian Museum; pp. 6, 11, 15, 26 British Museum; pp. 7, 12 The Art Archive; pp. 8, 17 Roger Wood/Corbis; pp. 9, 25 Agence Photographique de la Reunion des Musees Nationaux/Louvre; pp. 10, 20, 28 AKG; p. 13 Ancient Egypt Picture Library; p. 14 Scala; p. 16 Corbis; p. 18 Ancient Art and Architecture; p. 19 Trevor Clifford; p. 21 National Trust; p. 22 Bildarchive; p. 23 The Worshipful Company of Goldsmiths; p. 24 Metropolitan Museum of Art; p. 27 Archivo Iconografico, S.A./Corbis; p. 29 Associated Press.

Special thanks to Rebecca Vickers for her comments in the preparation of this book.

Every effort has been made to contact copyright holders of any material reproduced in this book. Any omissions will be rectified in subsequent printings if notice is given to the publisher.

Some words are shown in bold, **like this.** You can find out what they mean by looking in the glossary.

Many Greek, Roman, and Egyptian names and terms may be found in the pronunciation guide.

Contents

Who Was Cleopatra?

The name of Cleopatra is one of the most famous in history. Cleopatra (69–30 B.C.E.) was the last queen of Egypt. She was born into the royal family that had ruled Egypt for nearly 300 years.

Egypt and Rome

When Cleopatra was born, Egypt was a very rich country, but it was very badly ruled. The real power in the area was Rome, the center of the **Roman Republic.** Through her rule, Cleopatra fought to preserve her royal family and the independence of Egypt. At the height of her power, Cleopatra made even mighty Rome tremble. She lived an action-packed life, and died when she was only about 39 years old.

How do we know?

We know much about Cleopatra and her times because she lived in one of the most exciting and important periods in world history. Ancient **historians** have left us many written records. Much of the information, though, was written by her enemies in Rome. These writers describe her as an evil, **scheming** woman. Anything written by Cleopatra's supporters was probably destroyed after she died. Some of the most important information about Cleopatra was written by a Greek historian named Plutarch, who lived 100 years after Cleopatra. He, too, had to rely on the accounts written by her enemies.

◀ Cleopatra has always been described as beautiful, although coins showing her portrait may tell a different story. She is remembered more for her great intelligence than for her looks.

What did Cleopatra look like?

Most of the statues of Cleopatra were destroyed after her death, so we do not really know what she looked like. However, coins with her portrait on them have survived. These can give us some idea of her appearance. **Archaeologists** keep discovering objects that show Cleopatra. From these we can learn even more about what she looked like.

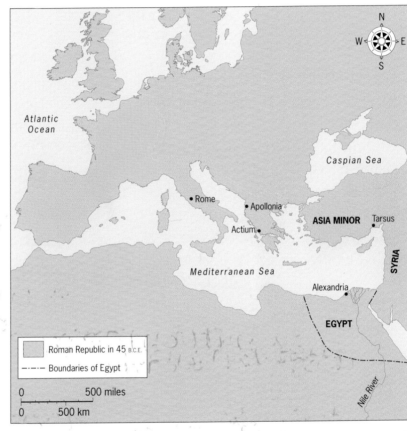

▶ **Egypt was a rich and powerful nation for thousands of years before Cleopatra was born. When she was queen, however, she had to fight hard to keep her nation independent.**

Key dates

305 B.C.E.	Ptolemy I starts the **Ptolemaic** royal **dynasty,** the family of Cleopatra
69 B.C.E.	Cleopatra is born
51 B.C.E.	Cleopatra becomes queen of Egypt
30 B.C.E.	Death of Cleopatra
	Egypt falls under Roman control

Watch the dates

"B.C.E." after a year date means before the common era. This is used instead of the older abbreviation "B.C." The years are counted backwards toward zero.

Princess Cleopatra

Cleopatra was born in the Egyptian capital city of Alexandria in 69 B.C.E. She was the daughter of King Ptolemy XII of Egypt. When she was born, Egypt was still a rich, **independent** country. Across the Mediterranean Sea in Italy, though, Rome was becoming more and more powerful. Many **nations** were being conquered, and the **Roman Republic** was spreading.

Cleopatra's family

King Ptolemy XII had many different wives. He had four daughters and two sons, but we do not know exactly who Cleopatra's mother was. She may have been King Ptolemy's own sister, Cleopatra Tryphaina. It was the custom in Egypt for the king to marry his sister. Cleopatra had two older sisters, one also named Cleopatra and the other named Berenice. She had one younger sister named Arsinoe. Her two younger brothers later ruled as Ptolemy XIII and Ptolemy XIV.

Cleopatra's father was not a good king. All the princes and princesses fought for power and influence. Egypt was growing poorer and poorer because it was ruled so badly. The people became angry, too, because they had to pay higher and higher taxes.

▶ Cleopatra's ancestor Ptolemy I was an excellent Greek **general** who served under Alexander the Great. After Alexander's death, he made himself king of Egypt, the first of many **Ptolemaic** rulers.

Playing a dangerous game

Cleopatra soon learned how to play the dangerous games that were needed in order to survive in such difficult surroundings. Even the life of a royal princess was not safe. If Cleopatra found herself on the wrong side of the game, she might easily have been sent away from Egypt or, even worse, murdered.

▶ Alexander the Great was only a young man when he set out to increase Greece's power. He conquered many nations, including Egypt, before he died at age 33.

Alexander's Egypt

In 332 B.C.E., the Greek king and military leader Alexander the Great conquered Egypt. He created a new capital city on the shores of the Mediterranean Sea. He named this city Alexandria, after himself. After Alexander's death in 323 B.C.E., Egypt was ruled by one of his generals, named Ptolemy. Ptolemy declared himself King Ptolemy I of Egypt in 305 B.C.E. His family ruled Egypt for nearly 300 years until the death of Cleopatra, the last queen of Egypt.

Growing Up in Alexandria

When Cleopatra was born, Alexandria was one of the most important and beautiful cities in the world. It was a great center of learning. Scientists, poets, and **philosophers** traveled long distances to study at the Museum, one of the world's first **universities**.

▼ When Cleopatra was queen, Alexandria was an important center of learning and **trade**. Today, it is still a busy city.

Growing up

Cleopatra was brought up in a beautiful palace with hundreds of rooms and halls. She and her sisters and brothers were looked after by an army of servants. Cleopatra did not go to school, but was given lessons by a private **tutor**. She was very clever and quickly learned many subjects, such as mathematics and poetry. She also learned to speak many languages. She was the only **Ptolemaic** ruler who could speak Egyptian. Most of her family could speak only Greek.

Ptolemy XII

Cleopatra's father, Ptolemy XII, had become king of Egypt in 80 B.C.E., before she was born. By 58 B.C.E., the Egyptian people were fed up with him and drove him out of the country. He fled to Rome, leaving his children behind in Alexandria. At this time, Cleopatra was about eleven years old.

▶ Ptolemy XII, Cleopatra's father, was a very unpopular king with the Egyptian people. It was only Roman support that helped him to stay in power.

Family fighting

When Ptolemy XII fled to Rome in 58 B.C.E., he was replaced as ruler by his second daughter, Berenice, after his first daughter died. Berenice did everything she could to keep her father from coming back to Egypt. In 55 B.C.E., three years later, Roman armies helped Ptolemy XII return to power. The Romans supported him because they wanted to have some control over Egypt, a very rich and important **nation**. He immediately had Berenice and her supporters put to death.

Cleopatra the Queen

Ptolemy XII was king of Egypt for another four years. He was still hated by the Egyptian people. He was kept in power only with the Roman army's help. In the spring of 51 B.C.E., he died. In his **will**, he had named Cleopatra and his oldest son as his **successors.** By law, only his son should have succeeded, but Cleopatra was too strong and clever to be ignored. According to Egyptian custom, Cleopatra married her older brother, who took the name Ptolemy XIII. They ruled Egypt together.

Queen Cleopatra

Cleopatra was now about eighteen, and Ptolemy XIII was only about nine or ten years old. The two hated each other, and quickly worked to gather their own supporters.

Because Cleopatra was so much older than her brother, she felt that she should be able to rule Egypt on her own. Although he was too young to rule, Ptolemy XIII had many advisers and supporters who did not want Cleopatra to have her way.

◀ Although Cleopatra was a queen, the Egyptian people worshiped her as a goddess. Here, she is shown as the Egyptian goddess Isis.

Not only was Cleopatra older and much more experienced than her brother, but she was also extremely ambitious. She was determined to make Egypt a great **nation** again. However, young Ptolemy XIII's advisers tried to attack her whenever they could.

As she became more powerful, they became more frightened. They were determined to remove her from power. This struggle went on for three years. Finally, in 48 B.C.E., when Cleopatra was about 21 years old, Ptolemy XIII and his supporters managed to drive her out of Egypt.

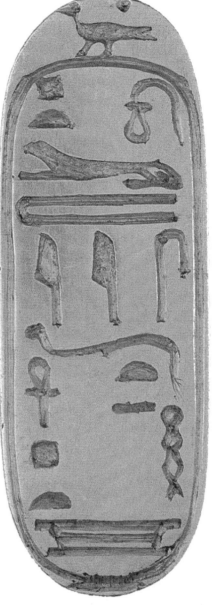

▶ This gold ring has the cartouche, or seal, of a **Ptolemaic** king.

The queen's enemies

Three enemies in particular drove Cleopatra out of Egypt. The most powerful man in the royal palace was a Greek named Pothinus. He was the chief adviser to young Ptolemy XIII. The second most important person was an Egyptian named Achillas, who was captain of the royal guards. The third supporter of Ptolemy XIII was another Greek named Theodotus, who was the young king's **tutor.**

A Dramatic Entrance

When Cleopatra was forced out of Egypt by her enemies, she fled east to Syria. There, she gathered together an army of her own supporters. She planned to fight her way back to Egypt and regain power.

As Cleopatra was preparing to march back to Egypt with her army, events took a sudden and unexpected turn. Julius Caesar, one of the most powerful people in Rome, arrived in Alexandria. Julius Caesar had sailed to Egypt to fight his enemy, Gnaeus Pompeius Magnus, known as Pompey. When Caesar reached Egypt, he discovered that Pompey had been murdered by his own soldiers.

More fighting

The fighting in the **Roman Republic** had ended, but another war now broke out in Egypt between the supporters of Cleopatra and the supporters of Ptolemy XIII. As the leader of the greatest power in the area, Caesar tried to get the two sides to make peace.

Ptolemy XIII agreed to meet Caesar in Alexandria, but he refused to allow his sister to return to Egypt. He threatened to have her killed if she dared to enter the country. Cleopatra did not accept defeat. She thought of a plan to outwit her brother.

▶ This Roman pavement mosaic from about 150 C.E. shows Roman soldiers beside the Nile River in Egypt.

A secret meeting

Cleopatra sailed in secret across the Mediterranean Sea from Syria toward Egypt. During the night, before the ship reached the coast, Cleopatra climbed into another, smaller boat and sailed quietly into Alexandria. A servant named Apollodorus rolled her up in a carpet. He carried her past Ptolemy XIII's guards and straight into the royal palace where Caesar was staying. The carpet was placed on the floor in front of Caesar. As Apollodorus unrolled it, Cleopatra tumbled out at the great leader's feet.

▼ These models show what Egyptian soldiers looked like before the time of Cleopatra.

The greatest power

The fighting in the Roman Republic between Julius Caesar and Pompey altered the whole course of history. Julius Caesar introduced changes to how Rome was ruled. Because of these changes, for the next 400 years Rome was one of the greatest powers the world had ever seen. Egypt would soon play an important part in these events.

Caesar Meets His Match

Julius Caesar must have been amazed when he saw Cleopatra unrolled before him. At this time, he was 52 years old, and Cleopatra was about 21. However, the difference in their ages did not matter. They were powerful, but they were also fascinated by the power and ambition they saw in each other.

What impressed Caesar so much was Cleopatra's great intelligence. Women at this time were usually not respected by men. Cleopatra expected to be treated as an equal, even by the most powerful man in the Western world. From their first meeting, Cleopatra and Julius Caesar fell in love.

◄ Caesar fell in love with Cleopatra, and with her **nation.** Egypt was rich with learning, **trade,** money, and beauty.

MT. PLEASANT PUBLIC LIBRARY
MT. PLEASANT, IOWA

The death of Ptolemy XIII

Caesar still hoped to bring peace to Egypt, but Ptolemy's soldiers attacked the palace where Cleopatra and Caesar lived. After six months of attacks, Caesar decided that he would put up with no more. His army defeated Ptolemy XIII's army near the banks of the Nile River. The young king tried to escape and jumped into a small boat. The boat capsized and Ptolemy XIII was thrown into the river. He quickly drowned, weighed down by his suit of gold armor. He was about fifteen years old.

Cleopatra was crowned queen again, this time taking her youngest brother, now named Ptolemy XIV, as her new **coruler**. Because he was only twelve years old, Cleopatra was definitely the one in charge—just as she had always planned to be.

▲ Cleopatra may have been young, but she was clever and brave. This ancient silver coin from Alexandria shows the queen at about age 24.

Blessed by the gods

The Egyptians believed that anyone who drowned in the Nile River, and whose body was lost in its waters, was especially blessed by the gods. It was very important for Cleopatra and Caesar to prove to the Egyptian people that Ptolemy XIII had not received this blessing. They had to make sure that Ptolemy's body was found and taken out of the river.

15

Plans to Rule the Western World

After the fighting between Cleopatra and Ptolemy XIII was over, many Romans believed that Egypt should be made part of the **Roman Republic**. Julius Caesar, however, agreed to allow Egypt to remain as an **independent nation**. It soon became obvious to everyone that Cleopatra managed to stay in power only because she had the support of the Roman army.

Cruising the Nile

Early in 47 B.C.E., Cleopatra took Caesar on a cruise up the Nile River, traveling with a great number of ships and soldiers. They rode in a beautiful royal barge, and watched the temples and palaces built along the shores of the Nile glide past them.

▲ Cleopatra knew how to travel in style. As her people watched her barge float by on the Nile River, they would have worshiped her even more. This nineteenth-century French painting shows how the artist imagined it looked.

◄ The Egyptians worshiped many different gods. They believed that the gods lived in magnificent temples, such as this one in Karnak.

Even though Cleopatra had won the battle against her enemies, there were still many Egyptians who hated her. She hoped that by sailing up the Nile with so many ships and soldiers, she would make it very clear to everyone that she was in charge.

Caesar's new plans

The cruise on the Nile was also a kind of public celebration for Caesar. New plans were beginning to form in his head. Queen Cleopatra was worshiped as a goddess by many of her people. Caesar himself was now the most powerful man in the Western world. Caesar believed that he and Cleopatra could rule a huge **empire**, stretching from northern Europe to the Middle East.

Traveling in style

Cleopatra's royal barge was very luxurious. It was made from expensive cedar and cypress wood brought from the Middle East. The decks of the barge were covered with wooden arches. There was a special area for Cleopatra and her guests to sit. Inside, the rooms were furnished with beds and cushions covered in beautiful **silks**.

Shattered Dreams

Julius Caesar stayed in Egypt for nearly a year. His **generals**, though, were becoming very worried that he was neglecting his duties in the Roman **territories** in the East. At the beginning of July in 47 B.C.E., they finally managed to persuade him to leave Egypt—and Cleopatra. He traveled first to Asia Minor (now Turkey), and then back to Rome.

Caesarion is born

By this time, Cleopatra had given birth to a baby boy, Caesar's son. She named him Ptolemy Caesar, but the people of Egypt gave him the nickname Caesarion, or little Caesar. Soon after Caesar returned to Rome, Cleopatra sailed across the Mediterranean to join him. She took their baby son with her, as well as her thirteen year-old brother and **coruler**, Ptolemy XIV.

▼ This carving at the Egyptian temple in Dendera shows images of Cleopatra and her first son, Caesarion.

Cleopatra in Rome

For the next two years, Cleopatra and her family lived in Caesar's huge **villa** on the banks of the Tiber River in Rome. Many Roman **politicians** were becoming very nervous about Caesar's ambitions. When Caesar demanded that he should be made king of Rome, they decided that they had to put an end to him. On March 15, 44 B.C.E., as he entered the **Senate** building, he was surrounded by a group of politicians who then stabbed him to death.

▲ This is what remains today of the **forum** in Rome. The main Roman Senate building was here, as well as other buildings such as libraries.

Making friends

One important reason for Cleopatra's visit to Rome was to try to get the Roman government to make a new **treaty** of friendship with Egypt. This would help to protect her position. With Caesar's support, the Roman Senate passed this new treaty quickly and easily.

Cleopatra Returns to Egypt

When Cleopatra heard the news of Julius Caesar's murder, she feared for her own life. She was so close to Caesar that she could easily have been the next person to be killed. As soon as possible, she and her followers, including her young son Caesarion and her brother Ptolemy XIV, left Rome for Alexandria.

Octavian returns

Another reason why Cleopatra left Rome so quickly was that Caesar's **great-nephew**, who was also his adopted son, arrived there. His name was Octavian. He had been completing his studies in the town of Apollonia (now in Albania). As soon as he heard of Caesar's death, he hurried back to Rome. He saw the young Caesarion as a threat to his own plans to take over Julius Caesar's position as ruler of the **Roman Republic.**

▶ Because Octavian had been close to Caesar, he believed that he was the one who should next rule the Roman Republic.

Back in Egypt

Soon after Cleopatra returned to Egypt, the young Ptolemy XIV also died. In Alexandria, stories began to go around that Cleopatra herself had the young king murdered. Cleopatra wanted her own son, Caesarion, to be made king and so increase her power in Egypt. It is likely that she really did have Ptolemy XIV murdered in order to get him out of the way. Caesarion was now crowned king. He was only three years old.

In Rome at this time, the most important person was a great **general** named Mark Antony. Cleopatra's enemy Octavian, however, was waiting for an opportunity to remove Antony from the picture. Octavian believed that only he should take Caesar's place as Rome's leader.

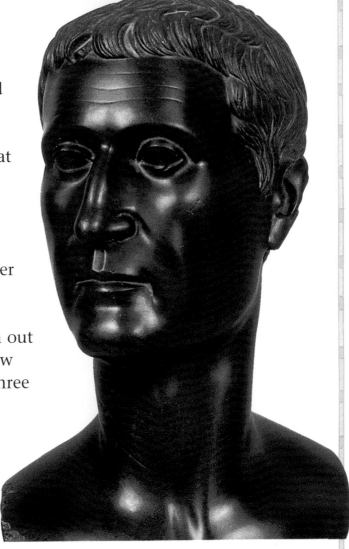

▲ After Julius Caesar's death, there was a struggle to decide who should be the new leader of Rome. Mark Antony, shown here, shared power for a while with Octavian and Marcus Lepidus.

Discontent in Egypt

Every year, the Nile River flooded. This was important because it meant that enough food could be grown. For two years in a row, though, the river did not flood. The Egyptian people faced food shortages and starvation. Most Egyptians believed that Cleopatra was a goddess with powers over the Nile, and they blamed her for this problem. She became more and more unpopular with her people.

Antony and Cleopatra

Power in Rome was now shared among three people: Mark Antony, Octavian, and another **politician** named Marcus Lepidus. These three were known as the Triumvirate, and they divided control of the **Roman Republic** among themselves. Octavian looked after the Roman **provinces** in the west, Antony looked after the provinces in the east, and Lepidus took control of the Roman **territories** in Africa.

Antony sends for Cleopatra

Antony left Rome to take command of his territories in the east. On his way, he stopped at the city of Tarsus (now in Turkey). From there, he sent a message to Alexandria ordering Cleopatra to meet him. He needed the support of Egypt to keep control of Rome's eastern territories. He also wanted to become Rome's only ruler. He hoped Cleopatra would give him money and supplies to help him. This was the chance Cleopatra had been waiting for. She wanted to return to the powerful position in the Roman world she had to give up when Julius Caesar was murdered.

◀ Cleopatra was a proud queen, as can be seen in this first-century B.C.E. marble statue. She knew how to use her power. When Mark Antony needed her help, she would help him only on her terms.

22

Cleopatra was not going to be ordered around by a Roman **general**, however. She was a queen who should be respected. Antony sent more messages ordering her to meet him in Tarsus. She ignored every one. At last she decided that she would go to meet him. She sent a message to say that she was on her way.

Antony meets Cleopatra

Some days later, Antony and his guards were in the main city square waiting for her arrival. A large crowd of people was also waiting to catch a glimpse of the famous queen. They suddenly began drifting away and moving towards the waterfront, while Antony and his guards were left alone in the middle of the square. Cleopatra had arrived, and everyone had gone to watch. She came in a golden barge with purple sails. She was dressed up as Aphrodite, the Greek goddess of love and beauty. The year was 41 B.C.E., and Cleopatra was now about 28 years old.

▶ Like Julius Caesar, Antony fell madly in love with Cleopatra. This tapestry from the seventeenth century imagines them together.

A dinner invitation

Antony was amazed when he saw the beautiful Queen Cleopatra arrive in her magnificent barge. He invited her to dinner in his palace, but she turned him down. She said that because she was a queen, he should visit her in her palace in Tarsus—and he did.

A New Family

Mark Antony must have been dazzled by the sight of the queen in her boat. As with Julius Caesar before him, Cleopatra had captured his heart. He immediately fell in love with her.

Antony followed Cleopatra back to Alexandria and fell under the spell of Egypt. He returned to Rome in 40 B.C.E., to marry Octavian's sister Octavia. In 37 B.C.E., he sailed back to Cleopatra. Even though he was married to Octavia, he lived with Cleopatra in Egypt for seven years. They went on journeys up the Nile River and along the coast of the Mediterranean Sea, stopping in many beautiful palaces.

Cleopatra's children

Cleopatra and Antony had three children. The first were twins, a boy named Alexander Helios and a girl named Cleopatra Selene. The third was a boy named Ptolemy Philadelphus. They were brought up along with Cleopatra's first son, Caesarion.

◀ Cleopatra and Antony's first children were twins. This statue shows Alexander Helios, named after the Greek god of the sun.

▲ This silver dish shows Cleopatra Selene. She was named after the Greek goddess of the moon.

In the year 34 B.C.E., Antony held a magnificent **ceremony** to give Cleopatra large parts of the eastern **territories** of the **Roman Republic**. Most of these lands had once belonged to Egypt, but had been captured by the Romans. Since she first became queen, Cleopatra had wanted to restore the Egyptian **empire**. Now she saw her dreams begin to come true.

Anger in Rome

Antony's behavior shocked the people of Rome. He was acting like a king, giving away part of the Roman Republic to a foreign queen. Octavian now saw his chance to destroy Antony. He had already removed Marcus Lepidus from power. He now spread stories that Antony had been bewitched by Cleopatra. The Romans knew that it was only a matter of time before Antony and Octavian would fight each other for power.

The Death of Cleopatra

For the next two years, Antony and Octavian watched each other carefully. They both knew that there was no room for two leaders of the **Roman Republic.** Sooner or later, they would have to go to war to decide who would rule.

In 32 B.C.E., Octavian declared war on Cleopatra. He could not attack Antony directly, because Antony was an important Roman. He could, however, make war against Cleopatra, the queen of a foreign country. He knew that Antony would protect Cleopatra. Antony raised a huge army. He then sailed with an enormous fleet and thousands of soldiers to Actium, on the west coast of Greece.

The Battle of Actium

Octavian's navy trapped Antony's ships in the **harbor** at Actium for many months. Finally, on September 2, 31 B.C.E., Antony's ships were able to sail out of the harbor to fight Octavian's navy. Soon after the battle began, though, 60 ships commanded by Cleopatra suddenly headed back toward Egypt. When Antony saw what was happening, he sailed after Cleopatra. Abandoned by their commander, Antony's sailors and soldiers quickly surrendered to Octavian.

Octavian chased Antony and Cleopatra to Alexandria. Surrounded and with few supporters left, Antony heard that Cleopatra

▶ This is the **prow** of a ship that was found on the seabed near Actium. It may have belonged to one of Antony's or Octavian's ships.

had killed herself. He had now lost everything. So in the noble Roman way, he fell on his sword and stabbed himself. But the news he had heard was wrong—Cleopatra was still alive. The dying Antony was brought to the queen, and he died in her arms.

Cleopatra was captured by Octavian's soldiers. Rather than become a prisoner, she killed herself, too. Some people say she was bitten by a poisonous snake. Others believe that she drank poison.

▲ This carving shows a Roman ship with its soldiers. Notice the prow at the front of the ship.

Why did they run away?

Why did Cleopatra order her ships to leave the Battle of Actium? Maybe she thought the battle was lost, and wanted to return to Alexandria to strengthen her army. Octavian later claimed that Cleopatra was a traitor to her own people, and said that Antony was a coward for leaving the battle.

After Cleopatra

Cleopatra was about 39 years old when she died. Her dreams of a great Egyptian **empire** died with her. Soon afterward, Egypt was conquered by Octavian's army and fell under Roman control. As she had requested, Cleopatra was buried in the same **tomb** as Antony.

The last queen of Egypt

Her empire may have disappeared, but the name of Cleopatra has lived on through the centuries. It still makes many people think of romance, bravery, and beauty. Cleopatra was the only **Ptolemaic** ruler who is respected as much as Alexander the Great. At a time when there were few women rulers, and when women usually had little influence, Cleopatra used all her skills to try to make sure that Egypt remained an **independent nation.** By doing this, she made even the leaders of the powerful **Roman Republic** frightened of her.

◄ For all her rights and wrongs, no one can deny that Queen Cleopatra was one of the greatest rulers of Egypt.

▶ Much of ancient Alexandria now lies under the sea. Little by little, archaeologists are finding lost objects.

Before she died, Cleopatra had sent Caesarion away to safety in India, but Octavian's spies tracked him down. The young man was murdered when he was only seventeen years old. Cleopatra's other three children were taken back to Rome and brought up as Romans. Cleopatra Selene later married the King of Mauretania. We do not know what happened to her other two children.

The lost tomb of Cleopatra

Over the centuries, the tomb of Cleopatra was lost and forgotten. Conquerors came and went. The beautiful city of Alexandria was destroyed and built over. Parts of it now lie beneath the modern city, and other parts have been covered by the sea. Recently, underwater **archaeologists** have begun to recover many statues and carved stones from buildings Cleopatra would have known. Maybe one day they may even discover the tomb of Cleopatra, the last queen of Egypt.

Glossary

archaeologist person who finds out about the past by studying the remains of buildings and other objects

ceremony formal event with special parts to it

coruler someone who rules with another person

dynasty family of rulers, in which power is inherited from one generation by the next

empire large land or group of lands ruled by one person or government

forum open space in Roman towns used by the public

general leader in an army

great-nephew son of a person's nephew or niece

harbor place where ships and boats can come in close to the land

historian person who studies and writes about the past

independent free from control

nation group of people organized into a single country that has its own rulers

philosopher thinker who tries to understand the world, the purpose of the universe, and the nature of human life; Greek for "someone who loves knowledge"

politician person involved in government matters

province area within an empire; for example, outside Rome but under Roman control

prow pointed part at the front of a ship

Ptolemaic relating to rulers who belonged to the Ptolemy family in Egypt

Roman Republic area of Europe and North Africa controlled from the city of Rome between about 509 and 27 B.C.E.

scheming secretly plotting to gain power and influence

Senate group of officials that governed Rome

silk expensive cloth woven from the fibers of silkworms

successor person who takes over from someone else, especially a ruler

territory district or section of land

tomb burial place, often marked by a stone or building

trade buying and selling of goods, such as food

treaty formal agreement made between countries

tutor teacher hired to teach a child at home

university place where many subjects are taught at an advanced level

villa large house of a wealthy person

will legal document in which a person says how his or her property and money should be divided up after death

---

Roman numerals (numbers)

The Romans did not have separate signs for writing numbers. They used letters instead. Here are the Roman numbers 1 to 20:

I, II, III, IV, V, VI, VII, VIII, IX, X, XI, XII, XIII, XIV, XV, XVI, XVII, XVIII, XIX, XX

We use Roman numerals after the names of kings and queens to show how many people of that same name have reigned before them.

Time Line

80 B.C.E.	Ptolemy XII, father of Cleopatra, becomes king of Egypt
69 B.C.E.	Birth of Cleopatra
58–55 B.C.E.	Ptolemy XII exiled to Rome
51 B.C.E.	Cleopatra becomes queen of Egypt
48 B.C.E.	Julius Caesar arrives in Egypt
47 B.C.E.	Cleopatra gives birth to Caesarion
About 46 B.C.E.	Cleopatra joins Caesar in Rome
44 B.C.E.	Death of Julius Caesar
41 B.C.E.	Cleopatra meets Mark Antony in Tarsus
40 B.C.E.	Antony returns to Rome; Cleopatra gives birth to twins Alexander Helios and Cleopatra Selene
37 B.C.E.	Antony returns to Egypt
31 B.C.E.	Battle of Actium
30 B.C.E.	Death of Cleopatra and Mark Antony; Egypt falls under Roman control
27 B.C.E.	Octavian becomes first Roman emperor, using the name of Augustus; **Roman Republic** become the Roman **Empire**

Pronunciation Guide

Word	You say
Achillas	a-KILL-us
Aphrodite	af-ro-DIE-tee
Caesar	SEE-zer
cartouche	car-TOOSH
Plutarch	PLOO-tark
Ptolemaic	tah-le-MAY-ic
Ptolemy	TAH-le-mee
Triumvirate	try-UM-ver-it

More Books to Read

Martin, Amanda. *Ancient Egypt: Come & Discover My World.* Princeton, N.J.: Two-Can Publishers, 2000.

Shuter, Jane. *The Ancient Egyptians.* Chicago: Heinemann Library, 1997.

Shuter, Jane. *The Ancient Romans.* Chicago: Heinemann Library, 1997.

Index